History's Hotshots

VIKINGS!
Fierce and Fearless Conquerors

Elsie Olson

Checkerboard
Library

An Imprint of Abdo Publishing
abdopublishing.com

abdopublishing.com

Published by Abdo Publishing, a division of ABDO, PO Box 398166, Minneapolis, Minnesota 55439. Copyright © 2018 by Abdo Consulting Group, Inc. International copyrights reserved in all countries. No part of this book may be reproduced in any form without written permission from the publisher. Checkerboard Library™ is a trademark and logo of Abdo Publishing.

Printed in the United States of America, North Mankato, Minnesota
102017
012018

THIS BOOK CONTAINS
RECYCLED MATERIALS

Design: Kelly Doudna, Mighty Media, Inc.
Production: Mighty Media, Inc.
Editor: Jessie Alkire
Cover Photograph: Shutterstock
Design Elements: Shutterstock
Interior Photographs: Alamy, pp. 6, 17, 23, 25; iStockphoto, pp. 20, 29; Mighty Media, Inc., pp. 7, 21; Shutterstock, pp. 1, 4-5, 8, 9, 11, 15, 27; Wikimedia Commons, pp. 12-13, 18-19

Publisher's Cataloging-in-Publication Data

Names: Olson, Elsie, author.
Title: Vikings! fierce and fearless conquerors / by Elsie Olson.
Other titles: Fierce and fearless conquerors
Description: Minneapolis, Minnesota : Abdo Publishing, 2018. | Series: History's hotshots | Includes online resources and index.
Identifiers: LCCN 2017944043 | ISBN 9781532112768 (lib.bdg.) | ISBN 9781532150487 (ebook)
Subjects: LCSH: Vikings--Juvenile literature. | Civilization, Viking--Juvenile literature. | Scandinavia--Civilization--Juvenile literature. | Scandinavia--History--Juvenile literature.
Classification: DDC 948.022--dc23
LC record available at https://lccn.loc.gov/2017944043

Contents

LIFE on a LONGSHIP

You've spent the last two weeks on a boat with 30 other men. You've been out in the wind, rain, and sun. You've slept under the stars with little protection from the elements. It's been weeks since your last warm meal. You've eaten only dried fish and meat.

Now, you approach land. You're tired from rowing, but you're also excited. You've been preparing for this since you were a child. You are in the best physical shape of your life. And you are surrounded by brave and capable warriors. You don't know what awaits you in the new land ahead, but you are not afraid. Like the men around you, you believe that the time of your death is predetermined. There is nothing you can do to stop it. So, you have nothing to fear.

As you approach shore, several men jump out of the boat into the shallow water. You gather your spear and shield. Then you rush off the boat into the unknown. You are a part of one of the greatest seafaring **cultures** of all time. You are a Viking!

CHAPTER 1

Who Were the Vikings?

The Vikings were **Scandinavian** sailors and **raiders.** They were explorers, traders, and warriors. Most came from Denmark, Norway, and Sweden. They were most active from about 800 to 1100. During this time, the Vikings took over European lands using force and violence. They terrified many people. But they also spread Scandinavian goods and ideas throughout Europe.

Although all Vikings came from Scandinavian countries, these adventurers weren't united by a single goal or cause. Sometimes they sought land and resources. Sometimes they stole riches. Some Viking groups even formed permanent settlements. Vikings

Vikings have had many other names throughout history. They have been referred to as Norsemen, Northmen, and Normans.

VIKING LANDS
AND ROUTES

MAP KEY

Viking homelands

Viking settlements

→ Viking routes

founded major cities that still exist in Ireland and the United Kingdom. They were the first Europeans to settle in Iceland and Greenland.

Vikings were fierce fighters. They could be **ruthless**. But they were also capable farmers and expert shipbuilders and sailors. The Vikings' fast and stable ships allowed them to travel farther than other European groups of the time.

Timeline

793 Viking **raiders** attack the monastery on the island Lindisfarne on June 8. This attack marks the beginning of the period most historians call the Viking age.

845 Vikings attack Paris, France.

853 Vikings establish the town of Dublin, Ireland.

874 Vikings create the first **Scandinavian** settlement in Iceland.

911 French king Charles the Simple grants Viking leader Rollo a section of northern France that later becomes known as Normandy.

982 Erik the Red founds the first European settlement in Greenland.

1000-1001 Viking Leif Erikson lands on the Canadian coast, becoming the first known European to reach North America.

1066 Harold II defeats Viking king Harald Sigurdsson in a battle near York, England. Most historians mark this as the end of the Viking age.

Leif Erikson

Leif Erikson was born in Iceland in the late 900s. He was the son of Erik the Red. After Erik was **banished** from Iceland for murder, young Leif fled with his father to Greenland. Around 1000, Erikson traveled west and landed on the Canadian coast. He named the area Vinland.

Erikson spent the winter in Vinland and returned to Greenland. Soon, more Vikings traveled to and settled in North America. However, the Vikings abandoned their new home. Historians aren't sure why. But the Vikings returned to North America for timber and trade.

CHAPTER 2

Viking Attack!

Most historians believe the Viking age began in 793. That year, Viking warriors attacked Lindisfarne. This small island off the northeast coast of England was home to a monastery. The monastery was full of religious treasure and other riches. It was also undefended.

On the stormy night of June 8, a Viking longship arrived off the Lindisfarne coast. Warriors streamed off the ship. The Vikings captured and killed monks. They dug up altars. And they took much of the monastery's treasure.

A man named Alcuin wrote about the attack. It was not the first Viking **raid**, but Alcuin's writings made it famous. The Lindisfarne attack marked the beginning of a Viking age that lasted 300 years.

People were soon terrified of the Vikings. This group's attack style was like nothing many Europeans had seen before. And unlike most other Europeans at the time, the Vikings did not practice Christianity. So, their **pagan** ways seemed strange to Europeans. Before long, Vikings had a reputation as the bad boys of the **Middle Ages**.

Lindisfarne is also known as Holy Island. It is a popular tourist attraction today.

Leaving Home

At the time of the Lindisfarne **raids,** much of **Scandinavia** was divided into small clans. These clans were led by chieftains. People survived by hunting, farming, fishing, and trading. They traveled by ship to trade goods overseas. Scandinavians had been **refining** shipbuilding techniques for centuries. They had the sturdiest, fastest ships in Europe.

Historians aren't sure exactly why Vikings began their expeditions and raids. Some young Vikings were simply looking for adventure and exploration. However, as Scandinavia's population grew, there was less land available to earn money on. So through expeditions, Vikings could gain land and wealth by stealing.

Chieftains led Vikings on expeditions and attacks. Certain raids had just a single ship. Others had hundreds of ships! European leaders often paid Viking groups not to attack their kingdoms. Leaders

even hired Vikings to protect their lands. In 911, French king Charles the Simple granted Viking leader Rollo his own kingdom. In return, Rollo agreed to become a Christian and help defend the king's lands. Rollo's land eventually became known as Normandy. Vikings controlled the region for more than 100 years.

Vikings often grew barley, rye, and oats on their farms. They also raised animals such as cattle, goats, pigs, and sheep.

OYAR 7.50 : FØROYAR 7.50 : FØROYAR 7.50

Gerandisdagurin í víkingaøld

CHAPTER 4

Exploring and Colonizing

Vikings were also colonizers. Swedish Vikings traveled east and settled in what is now Ukraine and Russia. Meanwhile, Norwegian and Danish Vikings focused on Western Europe. Vikings attacked Paris, France, in 845. Vikings also founded the Irish city of Dublin in 853. These warriors also controlled much of England and Scotland.

Other Vikings traveled even farther. Vikings made it as far south as the Middle East. In the 850s, a Norwegian sailor landed on an island now known as Iceland. Vikings later settled in Iceland in 874. Viking Erik the Red founded the first European settlement in Greenland in 982. Around 1000, his son, Leif Erikson, became the first European to arrive in North America.

By this time, life in **Scandinavia** was becoming more stable. Christianity was taking hold. **Raiding** went against Christian beliefs. In 1066, Viking king Harald Sigurdsson tried to claim land in

Hotshot Fact

Harold II was defeated and killed in 1066 by William the Conqueror. William wasn't a Viking. But he was descended from Rollo, the Viking leader of Normandy!

Vikings often formed permanent settlements. They raised families and built houses and barns on farmland.

England. He was defeated by English king Harold II in a battle near York, England. This was the last major Viking attack in Europe. The Viking age was over.

A Warrior Culture

Vikings didn't have any formal battle training. Most Vikings started their lives as farmers or traders. But weapons were common throughout **Scandinavia**. Most men learned to use weapons at a young age. They learned to hunt. Sports and games helped them learn to fight. Young men hoping to become warriors joined **raiding** bands of Vikings. That way, they could learn from more experienced fighters.

WOMEN WARRIORS

Few women, if any, participated in Viking raids. In fact, the Old **Norse** word for *Viking* only applied to males. But women still played an important role during the Viking age.

Scandinavian women had much more freedom than other European women of the time. They could file for divorce. And they ran farms and

Hotshot Fact

Even if warrior women didn't exist in the Viking age, they were an important part of Norse mythology. Valkyries were women who served the god Odin. They wore armor and helmets and protected worthy warriors on the battlefield.

16

There are many models of Viking settlements in US and European museums. These models show how Vikings and their families lived.

businesses. Some women even accompanied their Viking husbands on trips. **Scandinavian** writings about the Viking age mention female warriors known as shield maidens. But historians aren't sure if these female fighters existed.

CHAPTER 6

Viking Weapons

Weapons were an important part of **Scandinavian** culture.
And Vikings took great pride in their weapons. Spears were
common Viking weapons. A Viking spear usually had a
wooden shaft that was 6 to 10 feet (2 to 3 m) long. It was
tipped with a sharp, metal spearhead. Some fighters used
two spears at once.

Swords were another popular weapon Vikings used during **raids**. However, swords were expensive. So, they were often owned only by the wealthiest warriors. Swords became a status symbol. They often featured decorated **hilts**. Many Vikings even gave their personal swords nicknames.

Battle axes, bows and arrows, and shields were other important weapons. Viking shields were usually circular and made of wood. An iron dome in the shield's center protected the warrior's hand. Shields were sometimes lined with leather and may have had leather or metal rims. They were often painted.

Vikings may have mounted their shields on the sides of their ships when approaching a raid site. This protected the Vikings as they sailed in. It also inspired fear in their victims!

Viking swords and spears were usually made of iron. Sometimes they had silver, copper, or bronze decorations.

Sea and Ships

Viking weapons may have been frightening. But these warriors' greatest strengths were their ships. Vikings used two main types of ships. These were called *drekar* and *knarr*.

Drekar, or dragon ships, were used for **raids**. These ships were also called longships. They often featured dragon heads or other decorations. They used sails on the open ocean. They also had oars to use closer to land. These ships could travel long distances. But they were also ideal for shallow water near shore. They could even travel up rivers.

Knarr were similar to longships. But they were wider and had fewer oars. This gave them more room for cargo and passengers. These ships were mainly used for trading.

A Viking ship usually had a crew of 25 to 60 men. Larger ships could carry more than 100 Vikings!

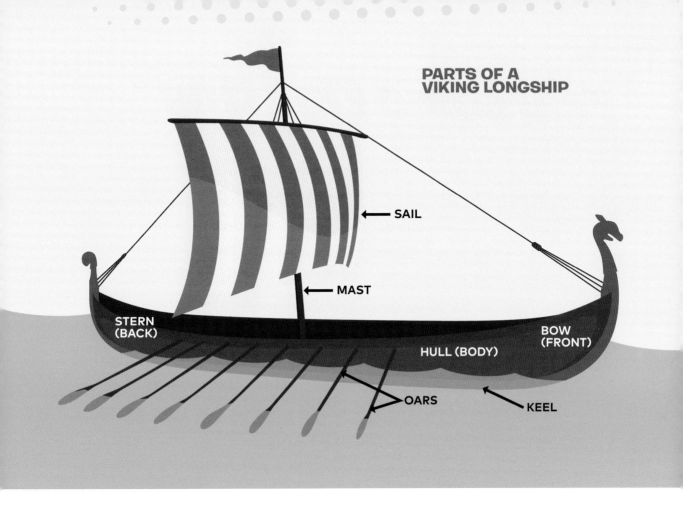

SAIL

MAST

STERN
(BACK)

HULL (BODY)

BOW
(FRONT)

OARS

KEEL

SHIPBUILDING

Viking shipbuilders didn't use plans. Instead, they built by eye.
First, they laid the **keel**. Shipbuilders cut planks for sides and
supporting beams. Wooden pegs and iron **rivets** held the ship
together. Finally, builders stuffed wool and pine tree tar into
any cracks or seams. This kept water out.

Fearsome Fighting

Vikings' ships gave them their greatest military **strategies** of surprise and **mobility**. These ships were fast. They could travel almost anywhere. But most Vikings favored less risky targets, like churches and monasteries. These targets were usually undefended.

Once a ship was spotted, victims had little time to prepare. Viking ships could be pulled up on beaches. This allowed the Vikings to unload quickly. Then they would steal riches, load the ship, and retreat. They were usually gone before their victims could defend themselves. Once at sea, Viking ships were too fast to be caught.

FIERCE FOES

Sometimes Vikings were forced to fight well-prepared armies. Then Viking success was less certain. Still, a Viking warrior was not likely to run away from any fight. Vikings began battles by throwing spears and shooting arrows from behind shields. Eventually, fighting shifted to hand-to-hand combat.

Some Viking warriors were known as berserkers. According to legends, berserkers howled like animals and lost control of themselves in battle.

Vikings focused on attacking military leaders. Sometimes 20 to 30 Viking warriors formed a wedge formation. The warriors then rushed toward the enemy, hoping to split up its troops. Then the warriors continued fighting hand-to-hand.

CHAPTER 9

Dress Like a Viking

Vikings on the battlefield were a scary sight. Ancient Viking skeletons show these men often had previous injuries or wounds. Vikings likely had many battle scars. Because of their hard work, Vikings would have been very muscular.

Historians aren't sure exactly what Vikings wore on the battlefield. But Viking graves have given them ideas. Some Vikings may have worn mail tunics. These long, armored shirts were made of small overlapping metal rings. Vikings may have also worn reindeer hide as armor.

In movies and TV shows, Vikings are often shown wearing helmets with horns. But historians don't believe real Vikings wore these types of helmets. Instead, Vikings may have worn simple bowl-shaped metal helmets during **raids**.

OFF THE BATTLEFIELD

Vikings cared a lot about their appearance. Writings suggest Vikings bathed once a week. This may not seem like often today. But it was unusually frequent at the time!

Off the battlefield, Vikings often wore knee-length shirts made of linen or wool. They also wore long cloaks in cold weather.

Archaeologists have found combs and tools that Vikings used to groom themselves. Carvings suggest that Vikings groomed their hair and grew mustaches and beards. Some Vikings even filed their teeth, adding **horizontal** grooves.

Clues to the Viking Past

Much of what we know about Vikings comes from what they left behind. Vikings' graves have given archaeologists and historians clues about Viking life. Vikings were often buried with swords, shields, and other weapons. Graves also included jewelry, pottery, and other items. Some Viking leaders were even buried in their boats. The more powerful a Viking was, the more goods he was buried with.

Many clues to the Vikings' way of life come from their writings. **Scandinavians** used an alphabet made of symbols called runes. Vikings carved these symbols into wood, rocks, buildings, and metal. Vikings sometimes recorded details about their **raids** onto runestones. These raised stones were also inscribed with poems or other information.

Scandinavian poets often described Vikings. The *Vǫlsunga saga* tells us much about the Vikings. These poems had been shared

Hotshot Fact

According to **Norse** mythology, warriors killed in battle would enjoy an afterlife in Valhalla. Valhalla was a great hall where the Vikings would eat amazing feasts and fight one another every day.

Viking runestones weren't burial markers or gravestones. But they were often created as memorials for dead friends or relatives.

orally until they were recorded in Iceland around 1270. Other written descriptions of Viking attacks came from their victims. Vikings were also described by other cultures that traded with them.

Vikings Today

Vikings left their mark on the places they conquered. Vikings often **assimilated** into the societies they took over. They married local women, learned the language, and raised families. Many people throughout Europe, especially in Scotland and England, have Viking ancestors.

Many places have Viking names. Caithness, a county in the northeastern tip of Scotland, was a Viking name for the head of a cat. Many towns in the United Kingdom also have Viking names, such as Whitby in England.

Fascination with the Vikings remains in modern times. In Shetland, an island off the northeast coast of Scotland, people celebrate the Up Helly Aa festival. Each winter, townspeople there dress up as Vikings. Then they burn a model of a Viking ship to celebrate their Viking roots.

People without Viking ancestry honor this group's culture as well. In 2013, the History Channel released a TV drama series called *Vikings*. The fictional series is loosely based on Viking history and features characters based on real Vikings.

The Up Helly Aa festival takes place on the last Tuesday in January each year. The next day is a public holiday in Shetland, so festival attendants can rest!

Archaeologists and historians continue to study Viking culture. New discoveries are made every year! The Viking age ended nearly 1,000 years ago. But the Vikings are far from forgotten.

Glossary

assimilate – to become absorbed into a new culture or society.

banish – to drive out or to officially require someone to leave a country.

culture – the customs, arts, and tools of a nation or a people at a certain time.

hilt – the grip and guard of a sword or dagger.

horizontal – running in the same direction as the ground, or side to side.

keel – a structural part extending lengthwise down the bottom center of a boat or ship that gives stability.

Middle Ages – a period in European history that lasted from about 500 CE to about 1500 CE.

mobility – the ability to move.

Norse – of or relating to ancient Scandinavia or its languages. These include Norwegian, Swedish, and Danish.

pagan – one who worships many or no gods.

raid – a surprise attack. The act of attacking is raiding. One who raids is a raider.

refine – to improve or perfect.

rivet – a metal bolt that secures two beams in place.

ruthless – cruel, or without pity or compassion.

saga – a long, complicated story.

Scandinavia – a region in northern Europe that includes Denmark, Norway, and Sweden. Someone or something related to Scandinavia is Scandinavian.

strategy – a careful plan or method.

Online Resources

Booklinks
NONFICTION NETWORK
FREE! ONLINE NONFICTION RESOURCES

To learn more about Vikings, visit **abdobooklinks.com.** These links are routinely monitored and updated to provide the most current information available.

Index